GRAVEN IMAGES

John:
Thank you
Mike Sutton
(My publisher
thanks you too!)
MfP
2/14/08

Happy
Valentines
Day —

GRAVEN IMAGES

POEMS

MIKE SUTIN

Edited by Shandi Love Thompson

SUNSTONE PRESS

SANTA FE

Sunstone books may be purchased for educational, business, or sales
promotional use. For information please write:
Special Markets Department, Sunstone Press,
P.O. Box 2321, Santa Fe, New Mexico 87504-2321.

Library of Congress Cataloging-in-Publication Data

Sutin, Mike.
  Graven images : poems / by Mike Sutin ; edited by Shandi Love
Thompson.
    p. cm.
  ISBN 978-0-86534-610-9 (softcover : alk. paper)
  I. Thompson, Shandi Love. II. Title.

PS3619.U884G73 2008
811'.6--dc22

                    2007048874

Published in

WWW.SUNSTONEPRESS.COM
SUNSTONE PRESS / POST OFFICE BOX 2321 / SANTA FE, NM 87504-2321 /USA
(505) 988-4418 / ORDERS ONLY (800) 243-5644 / FAX (505) 988-1025

DEDICATIONS

To my friend, Joe, who taught me that a form of faith is hope
and that whatever people can do, they will do.

To my wife and friend, Esther, for the cover design,
correcting commas, semi-colons and tenses,
and for valuable content suggestions throughout the
composition and publishing process.

To my editor, Shandi, whose cogent comments and persistence
brought this book forward.

To my publisher, Jim, who honors poetry by including poets in
his stable of authors.

CONTENTS

EDITOR'S NOTE / 10

PREFACE / 11

GODDESS-WOMEN / 13

Late October Run / 15
Space Race / 17
Shuttle Diplomacy / 18
With Joy / 19
Naked in the Sun / 22
To: Life's Purpose / 23
Heave Offering / 25
Fetal Female Earth / 26
Goddess of the Birth / 28
A Walk Below La Bajada / 29
Qualachupe (A Poem of Death and Life) / 30
Memories of Mirror / 33
The Woman Who Ran Down the Deer / 34
The Split-Off Female Mind / 35
Contra Costa Canal / 36

OTHER DIMENSIONS / 37

Give Your Heart to the Hawks / 39
Matriarch / 41
Spirits of the Season / 42
Endangered Species / 43
Steel Tubes, Wild Pig and Something More / 44
Miracle Needed Here / 45
The Garden of Eden / 46
To Arthur, From Guinevere, With Love / 47

Grendel's Dam / 48
Eve / 49
Miriam / 50
Let Us Stay / 51
Nail Drivin' Man / 52
Elegy for Phrases / 53
Set in Season / 54
Flanges on I-Beams / 55
In Praise of Slime / 56
Crossing the Bar / 57

GOD-MEN / 59

Omaha Beach / 61
Survival / 64
War Is / 65
Arjay / 67
To Walk the Waves With Arjay / 71
Memorial to Arjay / 73
Al Einstein's Eyes / 76
John Robinson / 77
Toward the Beach / 78
Marloweman / 80
Meet Joe Black / 82
Moments of Majesty / 83
Sex, Money & Power / 84
Why We Wept / 86

NOTES / 87

"Thou shalt not make unto thee any graven image, or any likeness of any thing that is in heaven above, or that is in the earth beneath, or that is in the water under the earth."

—Exodus 20:4

" . . . mankind is neither central nor important in the universe; our vices and blazing crimes are insignificant as our happiness. . .

" . . . the human race is . . . insane. More than half its energy, and at the present civilized level nine-tenths of its energy, is devoted to self-interference, self-frustration, self-incitement, self-tickling, self-worship."

—Robinson Jeffers, Preface, *The Double Axe and Other Poems*
(Original version, 1947)

EDITOR'S NOTE

At Sunstone Press, the project that has become *Graven Images* was something of an experiment in which we were all exploring new editorial techniques. Sunstone was prepared to give full authority over a text to an intern. For Mike Sutin, an already established and published poet to take a chance on putting a new manuscript in the hands of a student who had not even finished her undergraduate work required a tremendous amount of courage and faith on his part. For me, being charged with the task of shaping the entirety of another person's manuscript when I had not at that time begun to put together my own portfolio was exciting and challenging. However, I believe this collaboration has worked out well for all parties.

While I am sincerely grateful to Sunstone for having confidence in me and allowing me the opportunity to be an intern and work on this project, Mike Sutin himself has made this a truly wonderful experience marked by a great deal of openness, patience, and a willingness to take suggestions from someone young enough to be his granddaughter. Not only this, but he has also become the source of a wealth of information for me, not only in terms of sheer knowledge of the world around us and from that which came before us, but also in the way he conveys his artistry. He is a man of integrity and humility who calls it like he sees it in his own inventive way. For the several educations he has offered me during this process, I am forever indebted.

—Shandi Love Thompson

PREFACE

The poetic insights, prophesies and passions of an iconoclastic genius provided the authorial spirit and impetus to pull together this collection.

The poems of Robinson Jeffers (1887-1962), whose ideas have become so relevant to the 21st century, should again be appreciated and honored. Jeffers is attracting new attention from academics and aficionados. He translated into powerful poetry the actions and antics, the myths and mind, and the less than a grain-of-sand emplacement in the unending universe of unholy inhumankind.

Jeffers urged detachment from his reality as he understood it. Employing an independent dithyrambic and, sometimes, a certain measured rhythm, he used creativity of words to share his convictions. His work includes both longer narratives and shorter lyrics.

Most of my poems try to honor the past tradition of meter and rhyme. Jeffers would have dismissed this tradition. Aside from this, my poems do not always honor mankind. As for womankind, I have tried to let the expression of my feminine side emerge.

Historically, powerful goddesses were found where men were in firm political and religious control and such goddesses were reflected in men's images of women, not the actual power of women. I hope my poems do not so suffer. Women, being human, often share with men a lust for power over others, greed, envy, cruelty and aggression, not exempt from excesses of political zeal, ruthless competition, and a varied assortment of opportunistic, evil acts. I do not intend to differentiate between men and women with respect to non-humane acts. →

Consider for a moment the flip-side of the feminist movement of the 50's forward. Together with the positive achievement came the negatives. Women coupled opportunity with capacity to be equally recognized with men for cruel, opportunistic evil, exercised within or without the context of a position of personal, corporate or political power. The human animal is just difficult to understand.

In *Civilization and Its Discontents,* Sigmund Freud observed that humans are not gentle creatures: "[T]heir neighbor is for them not only a potential helper . . . but also someone who tempts them to satisfy their aggressiveness on him, to exploit his capacity for work without compensation, to use him sexually without his consent, to seize his possessions, to humiliate him, to cause him pain, to torture and to kill him. Homo homini lupus [Man is a wolf to man.]"

Scripture states, "And God created man in his own image, in the image of God created He him." Genesis I, 27. One wonders.

These poems play with the idiosyncrasies of modern-day Goddesses and God-Men, sometimes in seriousness and sometimes in jest.

To be a sane, plain-speaking poet in these absurd times ought to be okay. Ah! For the contemplative life—

—Mike Sutin
Santa Fe, New Mexico
2007

GODDESS-WOMEN

Late October Run

There are no aspens on Aspen Vista.
The once golden uplifting leaves have left;
the mountain is closing for the winter.

The route to the ridge line is slick in spots.
Icy pot-holes remain from harsh fall rains.
The road is snow patched and frozen in places.

I've got to move along pretty quickly.
The wind whips through my wet cotton jersey
and drains my body of welcome warmth.

My nose and ears and hands are numb and ache.
My skin is sweat-soaked and sensitive to pain.
I've got to keep gaining, to pump plasma.

My legs are sore, blisters infect my feet.
My back is rubbed raw from my fanny pack.
And yet, I'm pushed and pulled up to the peak.

Beneath my feet, the snow crystals crackle,
as I try to keep going without stop.
I feel that life is ebbing from my core.

Every once in a while I wonder
why I want to win this tough uphill run.
I pull up short; I wonder if I'm sane.

→

I need to top-out and end this long race.
To finish is part of the main picture.
To endure is my heroic woman.

This is the tenth month of my cycle;
these are the winters of my running years,
and I feel very cold and very old.

Still yet, I need to put each foot ahead.
My raw will and mind will conquer muscle.
I know now why I want to earn this prize.

Only I can give value to my life.
The only purpose of life is to live.
I wonder why I must strive to achieve.

This struggle is solely with my own self,
and this challenge is a celebration.
I will finish the course; I am alive.

Space Race

I often thought about what I would do
when I attained the age of eighty-two.
Keep busy, I thought, and be a good girl scout.
Now, they are slicing sections of my stomach out.

There ought to be a place to go and die,
where tubes are not taped from your nose to your thigh,
and purple needle punctures do not repulse your eye.

I know I have to go someday,
but, does it have to be this way?

By all accounts, I should not even be alive:
Dr. A consults with Dr. B,
who consults with Dr. C,
but no one ever takes the time to talk to me.

Green ladies make my bed,
blue ladies hold my head,
white ladies declare me not quite dead.
Each one: a very busy bee inside the hive,
servicing, now, my sullen spleen,
the offering of a shriveled queen
who, when I had barely reached thirteen
(when we are old enough to bleed,
we are ripe enough to reap man's seed),
should have dropped one more member of the race
and died, to not suck up essential space.

Shuttle Diplomacy[1]

Good God! Now NASA's measuring
the speed of sperm which swim and breed in outer space.
I pity the poor purple sea urchin species who both fall from
                    nature's grace
and prey to gurgling test tubes preserving the infertile
                    human race.

These guys can score more with a plentitude
                    of the right stuff
of the galaxy; as for me, I'm a supersaturated
                    surplus city,
and, thank you, I've had enough.

To break the outer layer of my egg,
proceed apace, sea creatures:
stay outta my face, get offa my case,
whip your tails, thrash your heads,
                              break a leg!

When I am old and no longer a fruitful seeded vessel,
I will not wear your purple . . .
to celebrate my newly wel-cumed sterility,
my freedom from spiny taps of sea men
seeking to sow fertility.

                              Signed:

                              girl urchin

With Joy

"And David danced before the
Lord with all his might."

                        Second Samuel 6:14

"So David went and brought up
the ark of God…into the City of David
with joy."

                        Second Samuel 6:12

always landing
on lily pads

twinkling
like lightning bugs
at twilight

peter panning boy
and the lost lads
tossed sky-might silly
in an inkling alien
aerial ariel glimmer

sprinkling spatial
golden glitter
across global milky ways

kind and special
tinkerbell hugs

→

replacing distant clasps
of hands

mind-expands happening
sans energy-sapping drugs

sugarplum visions
caress and erase
dumb decisions
from consciousness

dancing bright
and high on drink,
here and disappear
in an instant eyewink

reflecting refraction
of a faultless
prismed fantasy
of crystals frisking
on silvered mirrors

leaping like bands
of leprechauns
on greenish sands
of forgotten Irish
seashores

thinking ethereal
thoughts of joy
in celestial lands,
reason being
out of season

twirled through swirls
of cosmic trust
and confidence

never tiring firefly
flitter at once
at one with the world

Naked in the Sun

I'm bored with stand-up ironing.
My legs are sore-floored to poured concrete.
O give me steam encased in steel,
to smooth these sick Van Heusen shirts,
and feet as broad as early man's
to find firm footing for this upright stance.

I think that sales from door-to-door
or maybe high end bricks and land
will use the best of what I've got;
or, like a goddess of a golden age,
to sing like Circe's siren's sang
and peel and play all naked in the sun.

Then form a column base for hot Hyperion.

To: Life's Purpose[2]

Where once the he who walked the waves arms spread,
soft sandaled steps across the sands of time,
on sinuousities of ancient seas,
and women washed the feet of him and wept
for him who never shared his sainted seed
to perpetuate the extinct species
from evolutionary and unknown;
how can we now know where his seed was sown
or where upon the ground the seed was spent?

It is the street of Jesus where he went,
the Jerusalem road of stone once swept
by hem of woven scarlet robe,
the day star struck too soon at deadly noon,
too dark to want to live with mortal sins.
Our souls are not at home in heavens' spins.
The mind of man makes myths and gods to find
its being-ground, needs ego death and Vibram souls
to grasp the mystery of life; and only
un-man can mediate testosterone
and fear of being all alone,
or not at all, and passing, like a stone.

O unconscious cosmos, indifferent
universe, once venerable cosmic womb,
now cold and hostile hollow tomb,
how then has goddess mother disused us?
We separate at birth from her warm uterus
and wrench into a world without a womb.

→

The consensus is that we world construct;
reality is that we live to fuck
and fuck to live, for man has many lives to give,
one certain empirical foundation,
one secure ground for civilization.

Heave Offering[3]

When my woman's womb worked right, I knew
wherein my body one small seed grew,
securely, giving life. My life will surely die,
fullness flesh function thus fulfilled, my "she,"
my mythic man-child's heroic cry,
for cosmic evermore, eternity;
my re-birth engine body works might go awry;
he suckles at my swollen breast, nonetheless,
knows not never-never nothingness,
is much more marked by "I"
than mostly mortal me.

He will arise with holes in feet and hands of lime,
unmindful of in whose blue sky he lands, in rhyme,
shape-shifting through the sea-swept sands of time.
Who knows where my best and rest of life will lie?
He who heaved from out my thighs is my reality.
Unlike my son, I am all that I ever want to be,
while he survives to die and deify.

Fetal Female Earth[4]

O wingéd Pegasus,
in thy sky-flight, soul-soar to heaven's throne
and praise this song alone
among the disputatious gods on high.

From out the first vapid viral, vegetating
in the froth of heated, seething seas,
minute molecules of being moved.
Fleas-on-rats disease immobilizes non-inoculated man.
Pustules form from West Nile virus,
obstructing breath from stopped-up pores.
Plagues pour through the plebes
like vodka through a drunken duck.
AIDS tears through those who want to fuck,
fruitful fulfillment of serpent phallus.
SARS is spread by ferrets, cats and raccoon dogs.
The Lord inflicts on Pharaoh, frogs.
Malignant lung membranes form from inflamed fungus.
No gift from golden Venus these,
rising from the wind-washed waves.
Purple asters, apache plume,
golden pollen halo spume,
spray of juniper's fall fetus,
assail each sore and suffering sinus sneeze
and snot-filled nostril suffused by microbic breeze,
enough to cause a woman's constant cry.

Bile breath of beetles burrow through bark.
Asteroids, meteors, ruptures, release

heavy vapor shroud and urge the planet dark,
devour dinosaurs, eat the sharp-spined shark.
All merry men are meant to suffer
by machinations of the mother master.
Here is fetal female earth:
a blazing hearth of passion, giving trial birth
to beauty, as best as it knows how,
given goals good men will blindly disavow.

The greatest of these great gods' storms
are matched by vile and cruel man-can-do-it norms.
And to what end in human time —
honor, praise, to be splayed and split, or to the pit of lime?

Goddess of the Birth

While She walks, She watches distorted developing news:
CNN for poor revolts in Vera Cruz,
ESPN for holes-in-one at St. Andrews,
a Goddess gripping old cold granite of God-Man's World's
    subsiding soul,
a World where Women run from winter's rending wolves
and Men mind-worship, jealous of Her breasts and
    reproducing womb.
She runs from biologically based bad boy behaviors
and births war-warped wounded earth-bound saviors.

A Walk Below La Bajada

Arroyo walking was always at arrest today.
Snow froze to ice; Vibram soles could not hold to granite,
and darkness dimmed the glitter of garnets and micaceous schist.
Overcast clouds morphed from stalking grays to storm-roar
whites whose hail-stone hammers ground red clay dry core to silt.
Pounding rock-washed waters transported the after-birth of earth
beyond the stream bed of the wounded earth-born womb to artery's
    end.
We headed up for higher ground to watch how sky reigns over world.

Qualachupe (A Poem of Death and Life)

I promised I would compose
this poem of prayer praise
for Her, yet
protect the name by which
I know Her
and She reveals herself to me.

I have cried
and cannot sleep
when they steal our shrines
and raze the souls
of our people.

Let us dare not forget
the day of the dead,
for where else does the thread
of our bare lives lead?

We do not fear
the Good Friday procession
of death cart
rattle through the street
of our little villa.

La Muerte wears
a white keepsake dress,
a saintly habit.
A slight seductress,
She appears

at the head of the bed
near the door of the poor.

Something there
is about the heart
of lovely Lourdes,
at first sight rising
from a steep
valley high
in Mexico,
that you could
learn to love.

Her, with skin
as fair and tender
as a lambskin leather glove.
Devotion here
runs deep
like the dark
La Morena virgin snow.

Our Lady of Guadalupe,
La Leyenda Negra,
crushes serpents' heads,
and, for those, mostly, there
is no intercession
or caress.

I ache. Why now? Why me?
Pee ghostly yellow
on the white
and sparkling snow

→

nestled near
the Santuario de Chimayo
(or pink, I think,
or maybe blue).

She knew one
rendezvous,
nearly nine months
before the winter solstice,
when the rabbit
was snatched by the snake,
bled scary red and died.

Memories of Mirror

Yoda: Time again to lighten up, it is,
to tighten up my waist enhancing belt.
Oft of one wide expanse have I been told,
of abdomen encircled by loose stretch pants
and memories of mirror-reflected svelte
when trimmed out for the senior dance.
Outspread before the looking glass fourfold,
about to burst at birth the holy His.

The Woman Who Ran Down the Deer

The woman who ran down the deer,
she went to the west to make a new start.
She was the best there ever was, she was.
She knew the rocks, the rivers and the trees.
God blessed with strong legs and steady strides and fast,

she skirted past down-timber and scrub-oak root,
whirled upward onto hilly land too steep to plow,
steered a pursuit along a trail of droppings,
tell-tale sign of the red tail hart,
annual forager among the tall buffalo and grama grass,

all losing life in deepest fall
before the coming season's snow,
then pulled up short . . . still . . . pause . . . mute.
She did not stop until the deer dropped dead.
They called it the last harvest of the far west forest.

The Split-Off Female Mind

Come Thursday,
she stands wringing wet beneath
the Quailies' installed shiny shower heads,
a veteran of some seven miles of sweat
on mills of twirling treads
at a pace of eight; still, yet, her thought-space
is filled with millisecond threads
of weathered wreaths of fears and 'fraids, of doubts and dreads
of incapacitated parents and deflowered maidenheads,
car payment blues, monthly dues,
how to firmly face today's date of fitful shreds,
of time and money crunches that come and go,
ebb and flow, in beamed-up bunches.
The split-off female mind spontaneously sows and sheds.
O take us now to fanciful pillowed feather beds
where coverlets and spreads pull up to muffle consciousness,
offer grace, and silence troubled heads.

Contra Costa Canal

Avert thine eyes,
thy divine protuberances,
cast down thy soul,
maintain a sense of alert;
a pervert on the prowl,
a sign of the times,
may be ensconced along the route;
domestic water, do not pollute;
your long thin line is no defense
from the fly-by of the foul.
This canal is made for running,
but not for you.

OTHER DIMENSIONS

Give Your Heart to the Hawks[5]

Give a rush to the raptors, a jolt to the fledglings,
a great iron bolt of Jupiter's thunder, a hot line to the
     hatchlings,
to the upturned bald babies' beaks that squawk,
through the heart of the sharp-shinned hawk,
and hurry hard to earth in a world of deadly hurt.

Lay open the diurnal perching bird of prey
to ions of a gamma ray bursting from a cosmic layer.
Carry Enron electron energy to the pump
passage. Promote a volt to a vertebrate ventricle valve
and commit the roasted grey breasts to the deadwood dump.

There is no balm in all of Gilead to salve
the hot soup shot,
sapping strength from the venous vessels
conducted through electrodes to the fire of the gods of watt.
Beware the impulse of the power line. More
power through the copper wire to the people's holy pole

that, from its habitat, downs the plumaged predator
and the flying feathered family as a frizzled whole.
AC/DC electricity seeks the common soul.
Blot out the species, genus Accipiter. Civilization
is the cure for the nature god's creation.

Against the firmament, winged feathers unfurl,
riding like a drought dried thistle
whipped upon ethereal thermals whirling

$\longrightarrow$

like fevered dust devil dervishes prance
when delivered to high desert dance.

"We have come out of the drizzled-cloud coiled world,
more hawk than human; we had given our hearts
to the hawks to keep in the high slaughter sky;
Go up, wild bird, without a cry,
and bear it in lonely silence to the end of life."

Please, take this, my only human heart.
It's mine to give,
and with a spark it's yours to live.

Matriarch

Their great grandmère has gone to meet her gods;
to what reward is still a mystery of odds.
The almost unbearable burden of being a matriarch
has descended on me: I must save my family from the great flood,
like Noah's ark.
Yet, of equal force to them is my bite and my bark:
my unleashed tongue of platitudes
and prejudices of the past
depleted a world no longer fit to last.
I am now free to give advice that is not sought,
and my life's true worth is one less than aught.
My toothless mouth I use to nag.
My breasts no longer nurture, but shrivel and then sag.
The young ones now confuse me with the other.
With ease, my God! I have become my mother.

Spirits of the Season

There are cracks within the asphalt
where black ants have built a home.
There are holes in the soil-walk
concrete to protect the wing-less queen
who eats her eggs and chews off her victim's head.
Where, then, is the holiness of one
while whole hosts of ghosts of sainted-dead
and wingéd angels oppose the worshipping of one?
Out of the ashes of Asia, out of the fires of Africa,
when the sprinklers knock the needles off the trees
and come the swarms of fire ants, killer bees, disease on fleas,
peace means men's minds are placed on pause,
urges for idols etherized;
un-numbed, the need for kneeling's noble-prized.

Endangered Species[6]

Is that you, star-spangled girl?
Mother of the Maccabees,
down through the centuries you whirl,
last of an endangered species.

Manifested on metal highway signs,
image of a rusted rainbow,
sainted stains ingrain your shrine,
outlined in the rockets' red glow.

Saved by the corps and the bureau,
from hot, big river Hades,
swim silvery mirrored minnow,
last of an endangered species.

Aquatic backwater spawn,
Aztecan migrant manger,
latent political pawn,
born far away from danger.

Spiritual stuff is being owned.
From emerald backed inch fish
to backsides of green milestones,
God never meant you to perish.

Visions of Mary aren't scary,
and it's wrong to harass a fish.
While minnow ideas vary,
the Mother of God was just Jewish.

Steel Tubes, Wild Pig and Something More

Our ears, they must be made for something more
than unmuffled motorcycle roar,
like high-pitched death—scream of shepherd dog impaled
on naked knife jaws of fierce wild boar, or
souped-up 4 x 4s with metal pedal hammered
to black asphalt floor,
express-way for explosive, exhaust strokes
and blue-oil fumes soar —
smoke from corroded pipes
pierce our life force to the core.

Our years, they must be meant for something more
than tears and fears and biers and damning ears.
Some lives triumph like Tenzing's; some are badly botched;
in time, all bodies and treasured things are boxed
while cascades crash crescendos on some far seaboard.
Sea shell's coils are designed for hearing softer things,
like wafting waves' impulse that saturate the shore.
And here's what's meant by something more:
Only the distant sea shore always sings.

Miracle Needed Here

Can't you see that which now is so clear?
What we need is a new miracle here —

like another christ child needs to appear,
a man on horseback, like a paul revere,
a messiah, a pale rider, a jolly old
forest elf and eight tiny reindeer,
a cleansing wind called mariah;
a climbing webbed man called spider,
a bush burning brightly, a division
of paratroopers landing ever so lightly,
a cool yul leading the magnificent seven,
a miriam baking bread without leaven.

Whatever it takes, that's just what we need —
Let's hope that they soon get it right up to speed.

The Garden of Eden

What's good about a lowly weed,
the product of a random seed?
Produced by chance and random breed,
women and men have souls that bleed.
If I had been selected God,
I would have done a better job.
Had I a chance to play the hand,
I never would have planted man.

To Arthur, From Guinevere, With Love

The feel of my body is the feel of myself.
"The land and I are one" — A. Pendragon.
Better to quest for the Grail than for pelf.
But not today; I have a rag on.

Grendel's Dam

descended from demons, destroyer of danes,
sea-wolf, mere-wife, mere-wolf,
sea-hag, wolf-slut, wolfish water hag,
rag-on she bitch, raging sea witch,
blest in child birth, blessed called mother,
fury fem without fear,
foe foam on her full breast, her
head hacked from her carcass,
avenging her son, answering to none,
warring wo-man fame, wrong shamed without name.

Eve[7]

I often hear the serpent whisper-hiss:
"You know that Adonai Lord God will lie
to work His way with women just like this:
Eve ate an apple, but she did not die."

As Adonai Lord God commanded man:
"You will be doomed to die. Now I will drive
you from the gan, an eternal ban
from fruit you need to eat to stay alive."

He named her Woman; but man He did not name,
and he who had no name and formed from dust,
who had no spine with which to take the blame,
this mind-less one is not the one to trust

with wisdom, gift of life, or good and bad.
That Eve has never been in charge is sad.

Miriam[8]

She set him out amongst the reddish flags,
enwrapped in woven tribal rags
within a water ark of pitch and slime
to float the river's brink of thick bulrushes
and lulled him off to sleep with secret "shushes."
I stood afar to know what would be done
with him, but history did not write down
that which I did at that specific time.

In fact, I followed hard upon the chest,
suckled my bawling bro at breast
just like my mother did to stop his tears.

He was a goodly Semite child; we had our fears.
To save his Levite life from death or shame,
he never had a Hebrew name.
Not registered in sacred Seder story,
could there have been no Moses glory
in those unearthly ages hoary?

If so, no more a seer or prophetess,
I leave my cult converts in distress.

Let Us Stay

We're not so bad.
Let us sell silver
under the protective portals
of public buildings.
Let us ply our pawn,
paint pictures
of buffalos and bears
and dappled war ponies
on pots and pottery.
Let us barter and buy
blankets and beads
in a corner
of the market place.
We didn't kill Christ.
We didn't kill Christopher Columbus.
We didn't celebrate Christmas.
We didn't even have horses or cows.

Nail Drivin' Man

Jesus had a mother.
She did not have a Jewish name.
It would not have been wrong for Him
to have named her Miriam.
I had another.
It must have been pretty scary
to have had a mother just like Mary
who had no harpoon rammed into Her,
but who bellied up a carpenter
just the same,
a Jonah with a corona
but a real nail drivin' man.

I think about Him often,
with His dexterity to make a handsaw sing;
He should have built Himself a coffin,
a sort of unorthodox box
in which to be wrapped in a sheet of white linen,
because He came to Calvary to be a king.
But Mary put him a cave,
sort of a strange spot for a grave,
covered Him with rock and stone,
and then She left Him all alone.

Elegy for Phrases[9]

The looking glass gazes at the ghost face that has grayed
like a soul-stone inlaid in molten magma mush.
Blue eyes, thin lips inscribed the staged phases that his life payed -
out, slowly, like a trolling line of leadened weights.
Bound to sleep while tied in knots embodied by beds so badly made,
he failed to fuse with more than flesh, the way a female-woman feels;
he felt he left his life a foolish lie, alone, afraid
that he took leave with a pocketful of empty praises
for his lofty phrases and too much left unsaid.

Set in Season

The philosophers say that man
is mostly concerned with things he can
leave behind: his offspring or his works of art.
Are decisions made by well-armed dart
or by the "I ams" man can scan
by probing deep within his heart?
With all the fury fear can fan,
he knows full well he will depart
without a score, without a plan,
with little more than at the start.
Such things should be worked out by reason,
but yet, man's fate is set in season:
Activity is most frenetic
when he is pulled by things genetic.

Flanges on I-Beams

Jesus, my son, hand me the flange.
Carpenter, great nail-drivin' man;
when we adjust the specs and plans
and flex the minds of wishful Peter Pans,
we shall span the unconformity
reflecting bright I-Beams of eternity —
their sight scans as they deem to scheme . . .
the world the way I thought it ought to be.
Trust we can get it right this time for man.

In Praise of Slime[10]

In praise of ancient ancestors, we're here.
We are direct descendants of first life that stirred,
survivors of the atoms of eons and centuries
since first the face of earth was washed by ancient seas.
Culled out naturally to select a stronger species,
our lives are not our own at all but those of fools,
mere tools of complex mighty molecules
by which we must create new life before we die.
We live so long as to assure our lives will last,
an unending continuum of undulating
fertile egg and unerring sperm that knows just where to go,
not much more advanced than slow slime mold amoebas,
microscopic living oozy blobs, a self sufficient cell that throbs,
swimming through protoplasmic soup of primordial swamps.
A little lower than the angels is a long way from the sludge,
and "Made in His Image" leaves too much to mind's eye.
We do so-so with what we've got, but still we live a lie.
The immortal cell divides upon its co-enzymes,
but lines die, death derived, upon denial of end rhymes.
We've come a long way, genitor, but we've got far to go.
Not by might and not by power, some of many do survive.
No war, disease, or accident can kill us all to lose our lines.
We embody the being of beings from the beginning of time
and save the spark of being human on this unsafe sphere.
So far, there's been no breakage in our lucky link of life.
So long as God's day star will shine, we'll pull our slime
through time.

Crossing the Bar[11]

The sage observes: We all must go some day,
and so each end devolves on how and when and where.
Are those compelled to go their separate early ways
still aspirants for final passage prayer?

Sue would neither work nor wish away her inside ills,
nor master maddening mysteries
of life; she sought some solace in sedation pills,
loving lesser living through bare chemistries.

When seeking herself, her soul to hide,
to leave this circling sphere in peace with ease,
Sue thought of silent, scentless monoxide
and bought a second set of auto keys.

Sue wished she were a rising star.
The world, however, raised the bar.
Woefully wobbly her cerebral inner-states,
up on an Interstate, she walked into a car.

GOD-MEN

Omaha Beach[12]

I.

The night before the sixth of June, the sea was calm.
The lights of Flanders faint flickered from the channel flow,
belied the burnt flesh smell of blackened soot
egested from the charnel house.
A half a hundred years ago on a beach called Omaha,
in name of God and Fatherland, the best of both sides fell.
The greatest generation of young lives was lost to bullet and
    artillery shell
from concrete cliffs above, in a defilade defense through a deadly
    draw
positioned to inflict pain and injury and death upon an enemy
that inflicted pain and injury and death on universal innocents,
on those who were not equivalent to them,
in an inferno in which history records no lack of infamy,
in which the duty to dehumanize destroyed good sense,
events registered for remembrance by words of book bestseller
    Tom Brokaw.
That was a time and place the civilized condemn.
The bold aggressor head, an incarnation of a black satanic beast;
the adversary led by one whose dull esteem for life had simply
    ceased;
a dance of ignorant and gothic armies advanced by savage gnomes;
an augured choreography of discordant chromosomes.
The good guys bombed to bits in the French countryside
the bad guys who exterminated by genocide.
It must be nature's way to ethnic cleanse
the species homo sapiens.

→

II.

We live, well-tortured by our genes;
our future codes no other vibes.
Deep within each one of us resides
a darkened twist of tribal thrust,
a throbbing, aching surge of ancient lust
that never leaves but never hides,
that complements the fact that man must
always succumb to demagogic speeches,
always land on sacrificial steep pitched beaches,
to be selected throughout nature's aeons to endure
for centuries despite death's end and no detour,
to generate, re-create, replicate, propagate and clone
(so that our memory will never be alone);
without command or blessing, to bear fresh fruit and multiply,
from Paleolithic to Domini,
controlled by age-old organs that demand:
"The only purpose of your life is but to live from off the land"
(Winsome wisdom wrung from some lone chromosome).
To seek the thrills that pleasure gives,
we must submit to dominance and domino effect,
to slit the throats of thinly draped pre-women,
wan maidens wrapped in ritual and white ribbons.
Sacrifice insures the winds of war,
propels the fleet that floats toward land's far reaches,
where warriors wade ashore on sandy beaches.
Mere circumstance dictates our occupation with existential angst.
It is not clear to us to whom to bow to offer even thoughtful thanks.
Our intellectual landscape outstrips our ancient Paleolithic
emotional response that seems suspended in some static space.
In time, we may advance into a humane race.

III.

To overcome our fundamental thoughts of self,
our blind, unconscious, inside selfish drive
to reproduce ourselves and stay alive,
perchance by recourse to a better brain,
we can free our lives from nature and blind faith once again.
The grip of old gods grows weak with the sweep of time to reason,
when man's mind-probes mysteries are left to season.
Successive advanced ages will not fail to behold
the dying of anthropologic myths of old,
as if the god-head had declared itself for time delay,
allowing men the notions that men could move mind-miles away
(except for remnants of the past made part of allegory,
bobbe-mysehs, tales of yore, the moralistic story).
For it is not the genes that provide man's purpose evermore;
they disappear as generations birth and die,
from Abraham to Esther's Mordecai.
That which lives on but does not leap from girded loins to fertile
eggs are lines like these, these memes in mind.
Well sensored words will live in deathless bind.
The music of these meters, rhymes and metronomic rhythms,
will soon supplant the urgency of genomic algorithms,
and, in the place of prolix polysyllables of science,
short iambs will win out in fixed defiance.

Survival

I am sore-sick of guilt and shame and sin.
Nothing lives that God creates.
I am a semi-precious stone, insensate,
that fire-flames will lick to liquid state;
a cleansing seeks the peace of all alone.
Should we not build with iron, sod and stone
to make our firmament therein,
and not of cypress wood and oaks.
Surely all the land will in short order die,
if not of blades and axemen's strokes
then from finite furies of God's eye.
And yet, as long as simple cells divide,
some sense of life on earth will still survive.

War Is[13]

War is what we human beings are.
Where once twin beacons shone is scar.
One if by land, two if by sea,
signal lights for democracy.
New Ilium's towers are topless.
The City's void and unformed darkness.
Troy is sacked by Trojan horse,
and trickery by terrorist attack
has stilled the way to stay the course;
the ship of state is sorely racked.

Upon a once unbroken plain
in Babylon were built, with brick
for stone and slime for mortar, tall
temple-towers to storm the heavens
and wage a war against the gods.
Diversity of tongue has mystified
the one humanity to disunite.
There is a divide in the affairs of men.
Our world has known many Babels,
and we will win when we are able.

Lofty pylons, pyramids and spires,
set steel that scrapes the holy sky,
symbolic of man's high desires,
are vilely veiled, blind-sided, by
the jihad of the ziggurat,
defying diplomatic caveat.

$\longrightarrow$

For from the heights of history's towers
have hurled the hell of heaven's powers.
Raw war is what we human beings are,
brave warriors are our superstars.

Arjay

I.

Scalp Chief scrapes penetrating parasites from his swollen
body pores and straw-bed sores, a hot-rocks sweat-house
prayer in praise of lice and mites, of man-war vice, fueled from
the fissure-forge fed from magma forces formed far below
the Río Gránde gorge cataract, to cleanse the Winter clan
with night chants after summer's thunder sleeps, to rid the
third world-house of Taos of the chaos-ghosts and goddesses
emanating in emergence from the great blow-hole of the earth.
The laws of the Made People will not be ignored. He sits in awe
in the godliness of place.

II.

In dive-bomb descents like propellered Zeros, screaming siren-
shrill eagles claw at raw-pink rabbit flesh; black crows grate-
caw at fresh flesh conquest.

Shipwrecked stone red-eyed rats gnaw rotted flesh and issue
fleas; ice-age glaciers thaw the ridged Rock tops, cut deep
canyon cracks and recede through mastodontal draws, unleash
mulish man who hee-haws wise saws and modern instances;
meanwhile mind coughs-up gew gaws, jim-cracks, and
thingamajigs to heighten the capability for cruelty in the kill,
combined with human hubris to create great hateful hurt.   →

Corrupt kidney cells of chattering gang-caged chimpanzee simians simmering for primordial millennia, unsealed, set loose upon simple central Senegalese in cultured serum samples like a savage alien butcher bursts from out of Ellen Ripley's chest-bone, foreshadow a pandemic of genocidal proportions surviving for centuries, signaling the end of the era of the species of man who will from earth be cleansed.

Through the filmy morning mist-mirage rising off the Río Frijóles, the globe mallow orange night lights of Los Alamos lie sullen on the Pajaríto plateau like the serpent Python's ebbing ember eyes that flicker-on, flicker-off and . . . wait. What nature does not devastate, the nature's God instills in crownéd man to cut the head-count down; nature's way insures "no growth" in red-ash rhapsody.

The Nazarite sings of un-circumcised Gathic giants and slays with the bleached-white jawbone of an ass. Michal is delivered for one hundred flabby foreskins of the Philistines. No laws need play save Darwin's way. Man, he saw his Hiroshima, the hearthstone home of flaming flesh that sears and vaporizes like paint off melting metal, and: "I know a way to build a better ray of death. I beat my breast and build because I can," and said, "Let there be lights." And it was so.

III.

Summertime it is; Progress promotes rapid rewards in leisure living for martyred man who stays and suffocates in a surfeit of sins. Turn, little fire-wheel. He says: "I cannot" and, again, wakes to darkness upon the face of the deep.

The insignificance in the expanding universe, of puffed-up apish man: gypped by his inlaid genetics; betrayed by goading genitals; powerful pinnacled peaks perish, atoms of a grain of sand, ground like mountain river drainage roar gut-grinding granite Rock, generating greying Waters off the ocean shore of morning by the projected, but inhuman, God of Air, like glowing galaxies, lightning bug pinpricks, ganging up at night, flying to fatal fate like moth to flame — erased; desiccated incarnate gases evaporating like Asian ocean mist and floating free to infinite firmament; fires of the fear-flesh in final flight.

No great voice looms; no soul immortal soars toward a Savior-Superior; no visions are — the God of truth and things of beauty lives. No giant genies jump from thrice-rubbed jars to justify the pain of hate, the joy of kill, the endless death of all.

IV.

Pity poor man, pursuing perverse for pleasure, wallowing in the weakness of wasted worldly wanderings; his mind mucks in the putrid ooze of decaying murky marshes.

Human hearts are hardly highest in the gene chain when anchored in the feeling, feverish, and often fervent, brain; his pursuit of pain and joy pulses at the core, an imperfect freak of nature, evolutionary fluke, a fondling of his fears, forced to courses fractured like an earth crust fault by phantasmorgic fantasies of more.

How could the universe not attach affinity to he who nature worships and nourishes, most fragile flower of the firmament and of infinity? The God will not abhor itself.

→

Oh race of man, be mindful of the conscious, constant, colliding, all-consuming cosmos-king domain that does not die, creates ceaseless circles in the deep space sky, re-births all earths anew. And in the end, transcend, then, to certain communion, absorbed within the storm cloud swarm of swirling dust and ash of opaque evermore.

V.

"In the house made of dawn, in the house made of the evening twilight, in the house made of dark cloud, happily may she walk.

In beauty may she walk, with beauty above her, she walks with beauty all around her, she walks with beauty it is finished, with beauty it is finished." —Navajo chant, traditional.

To Walk the Waves with Arjay

I would have liked to walk wild-eyed waves with Him who wrote
of savage sea waters, seething trees, steep summits
and other permanents of note.
But as for Man, alas, He had not much good to say.
Ah, Man, not for all of time, but having only yesterday.

Cut into a golden apple, the core will quickly stain.
The core of upright animals unburdens only pain
and, with an inborn curse of cruelty that never stops to flourish,
engorged, abetting breasts extrude nippled milk to nourish,
suckled by satanic sons that only mothers could adore.

His brow was hardlined,
like underscore
upon a page of print produced by micro-processor,
muscular jaw jerked taut to taciturn,
and what He taught — uptight and sadly stern,
He knew that all of nature would at last soon crash and burn
but would renew, reflexively rewind.

Displaced plates gyrate, like gristle in the vitals grate and grind;
tidal waves smash shore line stores as if washed by giant oars.
Like ejaculate of molten rocks and melting stones reshape the
    seascape,
He spate a title wave of tilted words of lore
that rocked the storied world of poets' words.   →

His countenance was craggy-peaked,
pinnacled like pinched pie crusts,
but not crotchety-unkind.

Along the sinuosities of sea's shore line,
He would have taught me lots to learn,
of rapes and ravages and things,
and would not have left me very far behind.

His mind plays out like weighted cat gut line.
His words unwind, unreel, reveal reality,
but like a kitten teases twine,
a beauty plan of paradise for life on earth
with all the openness of Eden.

Memorial to Arjay

I.

Every single life has special value
to the momentary mental images
in the minds of men whose life the victim met,
but when lost to memory of loved ones,
no life sustains, good purpose is served, nada.
The little child at play in all of us is lost too soon;
a day that's past is lost and gone forever,
like forty-niner miner's daughter Clementine.
For, martyrs and kings, gods and generals,
sultans of swat and stars of celluloid,
great men and mountains, certain saviors,
are inscribed for memory in clay and cuneiform,
pyramids and pinnacles, the history wrecks
of human life, remembrances, monuments, memorials.
Not so, for women, children, peasants, proles.
Where are the skulls and bones and souls
of many million martyred men?
Their lives, ordered for three score years and ten,
lie like sacks of cement in the psyches of their kin.

$\longrightarrow$

II.

The who-sound of the great horned owl,
the cooing of the wharf-bound graying purple pigeons
among the rafters of the pylons of the dying pier . . .

It's only a jot of jagged granite rock,
a worn blob, a frosted bit of greenish glass
washed up upon the water's shore.

With the passing of the time of each man-year,
all shattered brownish bottle shards will grind away
like grains of sand
and leave no trace of human hand.

Good lord, Arjay, it's really only eons,
nothing more; only you could right the wrongs
and make it something more.

III.

Hawk Tower cannot be climbed in thongs
or slick-soled leather sandals.
They cannot grip the water-rounded river rock
rolled up from cliffs and coves that lay beyond the decayed dock,
tossed out by deep trench ancient avalanches
that bury bay's wide seaweed ranches.
(His work boots grip the gables of the world, gaunt stones
to haunt the home and hearth his labor owns.)
No thick forged-iron chain-link third floor handles
can provide good purchase for the headland tourist tide
on stepping stones cemented for a pagan Giant's long

and stately stride;
builder-creator of parables, epics, cycles, fables
wrested from God's gate tower Babels,
from staple tales of Vikings, Visigoths and Vandals
and episodic residues of dark Teutonic ocean lore;
O, we could light a thousand votive candles
to He who could make it so much more.

Al Einstein's Eyes[14]

Al Einstein's eyes are locked inside a safety box . . .
separated spatially from his fissured bottled brains
with slivers slight delivered up as studied curiosities.
From his blind, old, urned ash remains,
his entire self and soul will never reach intact
the pearly gated plains of Princeton,
the holy happy hunting grounds of gods;
his, an inflationary universe in flight, relatively speaking,
who never wholly sleeps in peace at night.

But Arjay wrote: "The peace of the dead is dearer than gold,
no one can rob you." He lied.

And all those who remembered his good mind have died,
his memory awash in ages, like Jimmy Jay,
wiped out on the barnacled boulders of New Brighton Beach
while waiting to board the wonder wave of silver surf,
just off the fog-bound bay of Monterey.

John Robinson

A brain that pulses with pure pain,
a mind that grinds against the grain,
who heaves against the hurricane,
twin lobes that tug against the tide,
mind-blinded by the monkey-mane
of man . . .
and in which calm cannot abide.

Toward the Beach[15]

I.

William Wordsworth—
Wouldst that thou were with us at this hour!
The freeway has its exits and its entrances
and each truck stop has many tacts
to lure travelers with taco tastes,
tamale pies, tortillas and french fries,
its easy-ons and easy-offs—
and all of them have food that's fried with fat;
the nation's arteries are clogged with fare that's fast.
The blood that's tired comes in late and last.
I tire much of travel and its futile hastes,
of eating rapidly and its attendant body wastes.
From much of this my tired mind doth cower.

II.

When I am old, I shall grow a flower
for my long flowing hair, and, bearded like a bard,
with all the rage within my aging heart,
shall push a purloined grocery shopping cart
compacted with pillow, hooded cotton pull-over
and a day's staples packed in plastic bags,
like a Latino in Pasadena's promised paradise,
and go out, an hour after dawn, among the people,
a pedestrian in opposition to gas propulsion,
along the dreary gray Pacific coast wharf-walks
(except where prohibited by public law)

and collect coins and uncorroded cans, and contemplate,
upon two broke-down tables of slabby slate,
our consecration as among the many constellations
of the Milky Way, and puff a pack of smokes a day
and wash ashore some day along the bay at Monterey.

III.

I am no more a fluent front page sage,
no longer full of wise saws or modern instances,
but I know my way around Park Place
and all the virtues of my private space.
I shall throw my internet among the sand flies near the shore
and ask for little and no more.
I cast no more for souls of men or fiber fiche;
My feet avoid the squish of gelatinous jellyfish.
I know too soon that I must sleep,
low batteries announce by not so subtle strident beep.
This life would drive the minds of most men mad
and, if so, cannot be so very bad.
We don't need no stinking seagulls creeping on
our bleeping seaweed weeping beaches.
We never saw no birds that bleed
awash upon the tides with bones less thick
than the leg of a chicken or a mint tooth pick.
And, in the end, we all are floating feathers
and cotton puffs of down upon a sea of sticky sand,
having failed to fully fathom the web-work of this land.

Marloweman

I want to be a European man,
freed of priests and popes
and papal English land,
proud to be a part of pagan
past again,
and free of fears of God
and full of hopes
for Man the animal.
To America, transport
pilgrim protestants, protective
of religious slaving strictures
seeping like insidious sewage
from stultifying scriptures.

Where is that new age
once welcomed by the intellect
and now incorporated wholly in
what Christians call first sin?
Cannot the cosmos cause defect,
for instinct cannot pace with mind,
that kills with cunning, a self conceit
in the plan divine,
and that is why we're in the sin we're in.

For if creator knew it all,
like just how fast and far we'd fall,
if creator had just known enough,
why weren't we made of sterner stuff?
Man can, and so, with arrogance,

he freely acts,
inflicts hacks both ways from double-edgéd axe
through flesh and fears and two-faced facts,
the razor blade of life's tap dance,
with no remorseful side-wise glance.

Meet Joe Black

I'd like to leave this world without regret,
for even fabled featured films will fade
and never be restored to former fame,
and all in time the tape goes blank.
My life's not long ahead of me,
I go to Meet Joe Black.
Remember me
and, at fate's fork, don't fret.
When it is time for me to split,
I'm not the guy who goes, I am Brad Pitt.

Moments of Majesty[16]

Santa Fé City's creeping Spring street service
applies quick asphaltic mixture fixes
to each glacially carved deep dish pothole
formed from ices and high sky's barometric mixes.
Oil of asphalt, essence of H_2O, repel in strife,
eat out the heart of traffic's swishy hiss.
A Karmic culture-crisis cured upon the Tarmac of hectic life
perpetuates and transmigrates my car-jarred dark departed soul.
No poet sings cathartically of skids, but kiddies,
not of double axles shirred or pneumatic tires nailed
by sharpened edges of a world of streets impaled
upon a want of permanence of progress.

Sing now of wheels propelled by
moments of mankind's majesties,
set hard against realities of stress
compelled by eons of emerging erectus,
sink holes and cement concrete heaped high upon us.

Sex, Money & Power

For to force-feed the famished family,
sprung rhythm from my lunging loins,
I scrape the city's concrete corridors
in search of country's current coins.
I am become a sole street walker,
a loathsome lost-coin stalker,
picking copper Lincoln pennies from clogged culverts,
like salmon anglers capture frenzied fish,
or separating stem cells from a Petrie dish,
while dodging Rams careening down the Drive
past Alamo, rattling like a wrecking yard
where detached truck parts get old and die,
lurching over cement curbsides seeking human flesh,
swaying side to side, wreaking havoc
with Tarmac non-riders, slogging
along the narrow channel's footways.
In Santa Fé, each walk-way stroller ducks and prays.

An angry engineer of this un-commanded run-away train
on whose parade my pesky presence pledges rain,
with rancor shouts and sirens sound: "Get outta th' street!!!"
But in obeisance to my abiding beat
of stalking the city's unsafe paths, I refrain.
For walks are of uneven pocked-marked
concrete rock, like an acned pit-faced kid,
a lunar landscape, waiting for an icy skid.
Reply I: "Take a hike, you mother fucker.

Impede not thy mortal coinage plucker,"
the urge to mutter more contained,
flip a bird
and take to gutter once again.

In the beginning of this troubled world
was the ill-bred word.
An avalanche of tonnaged trucks attacks
the refuse of the pocket and the purse
with heavy tire tracks; the curse
of snow, dust, crumbled, dried, cracked leaves
and mud makes murky mush.
Each double axle bobs and weaves
and hurtles like a Nike swoosh
to knock me off my fleeing feet.
This nation is undone by Patriot putsch.
The mint casts no coins for either Bush.
Shine perishing Republicans.
Insight our way to specie.
Illuminate the chicken feed.
Fill our pockets with what we need.
The Reagans of the world will fade to corporate greed.
The pagans' flag's unfurled in fury.
Shine perishing Americans.

Why We Wept

Why does white excite the sighting eye?
Tsikomo sits astride a sea of fog,
in dawn light, pink, at night, in +6ink,
which coats its creek bed coasts with pearl-like film,
like dripping low-float clouds enshrine the sky
and soak the Center of the World of All.

Before carbon dioxide dissolves the summit-barren crystal snow
and arctic Colorado Columbine and alpine flowers grow
in subtle shades of lavender to blue to white, and yellow too,
Tesuque Horse will hide its Head, so lost among
the forest's sorrow-song — scarred ski runs
carved bald from fir and cleansing fire high

up on the swollen slopes where lifts and eagles fly.
Sangre de Cristos washes out with reddish cold,
and gray mist shrouds the frozen face
of the weathered waters of Meribah,
where once we wept and wondered why
all men strike rock and know that they will die.

NOTES

1.

"Spiny sea creatures the size of doughnut holes will play an
important part in a space shuttle experiment next year that might
help answer whether zero gravity would affect reproduction in
space." — The Associated Press

2.

"She hears, upon that water without sound,/ A voice that cries
'The tomb in Palestine,/ Is not the porch of spirits lingering./ It is
the grave of Jesus, where he lay.'" *Sunday Morning*, Wallace Stevens

"So sinks the day star in the Ocean bed . . . Through the dear
might of him that walked the waves" *Lycidas*, John Milton

"He didn't walk on the water. He didn't multiply the loaves and
fishes. And he didn't change water into wine . . . " *Book Concludes
Jesus Performed Few Miracles, The Santa Fe New Mexican.*

"The purpose of life is to live." — Mike Sutin

"I live to fuck." — Harley Davidson motorcycle rider's leather
jacket back, Paseo de Peralta and Cerrillos Road, Santa Fe, New
Mexico.

"Gnats live to mate," explains Kent State University entomologist
Benjamin Foote. "Their only purpose is to pass their genes to
the next generation . . . I estimate 10 to 20 percent of the males
accomplish their goal." *The Wild File*, Stephanie Gregory, *Outside.*

"For Kant had drawn attention to the crucial fact that all human
knowledge is interpretive. The human mind can claim no direct
"mirrorlike" knowledge of the objective world, for the object

it experiences has already been structured by the subject's own internal organization."

"Grof found that the deepest source of psychological symptoms and distress reached back past childhood traumas and biological events to the experience of birth itself, intimately interwoven with the encounter with death." *The Passion of the Western Mind*, Richard Tarnas

3.

"And thou shalt sanctify . . . the thigh of the heave-offering . . . for it is a heave-offering from the children of Israel of their sacrifices . . . even their heave-offerings unto the Lord." Exodus 24: 27-28

4.

"Cats and ferrets can carry the SARS virus . . . The virus has been found in ferret badgers, masked palm civets and raccoon dogs in China . . . " *Cats and Ferrets May Contribute to Spread of SARS, The Albuquerque Journal.*

"The Senate rejected a plan . . . to curb global warming . . . a bill . . . that would reduce emissions of carbon dioxide and other greenhouse gases from industrial smokestacks . . . " *Senate Rejects Plan to Curb Global Warming, The Albuquerque Journal.*

"An asteroid or comet tops the list of suspects for the sudden extinction of half of all species about 200 million years ago, and another may have exterminated the dinosaurs 65 million years ago . . . An asteroid that size (one kilometer) doesn't sound so big, but when hitting the earth at 25,000 to 50,000 miles per hour, the heat, smoke and debris could alter the climate and destroy crops, resulting in hundreds of millions of deaths . . . " *Scientists Say Asteroid Could Hit Earth, The Albuquerque Journal North.*

"The sun belched another huge cloud of highly charged particles toward Earth on Wednesday afternoon . . . The solar outbursts . . . also include radiation from protons moving at near the speed of light . . . " *Sun Spews New Wave At Earth, The Albuquerque Journal.*

"We exist at the whim of nature. We're getting reminded about that. We are not the masters of the world; we're just living in it . . . " *Fires Show We're Not 'Masters of the World, The Santa Fe New Mexican,* Denise Kusel, quoting Gail Haggard, owner of Plants of the Southwest about the fires in Southern California.

"And the Lord did according to the word of Moses; and the frogs died out of the houses, out of the courts, and out of the fields. And they gathered them together in heaps; and the land stank," Exodus 8:9-10.

"The total worldwide count (influenza deaths as World War One was coming to a close) ranged between 20,000,000 and 40,000,000 . . . Smallpox . . . killed 500 million people in the 20th century alone, and infected one-tenth of all humans since the first agricultural settlements around 10,000 B.C . . . . HIV-AIDS now infects more than 40,000,000 worldwide and killed over 3,000,000 in 2001. Malaria kills 3,000 per day, over 1,000,000 per year in Africa alone . . . " *Allocating Risks of Terrorism and Pandemic Pestilence Force Majeure for an Unfriendly World, The Construction Lawyer.*

"He (Pope John Paul II) is telling people something he has believed his entire life: Suffering is part of the human condition." *Pontiff Seems To Embrace Suffering as Message to World, The Sunday Albuquerque Journal.*

5.

". . . the whole family of Cooper's hawks was killed except for one hatchling. Stodgel found the electrocuted birds at the base of an old power pole . . ." 'We love it when people call us,' said [the] environmental scientist for [the Public Service Company of New Mexico]. 'We'll come out and check it out.'" *Birds on a Wire, The Santa Fe New Mexican.*

6.

"The Rio Grande silvery minnow, a 3 inch fish of mirrored sides and an emerald back, was listed . . . as a federal endangered species . . . This means no one may harass, pursue or harm the fish . . . [T]he designation could have an impact on plans by the U.S. Army Corp. of Engineers and the Bureau of Reclamation . . . irrigation diversions left roughly 1,000 silvery minnows stranded and dead on dry riverbed." *Suit Seeks Safe Home for Minnow, The Albuquerque Journal North.*

"The rainbow images of Mary being seen on two highway signs . . . bear an unmistakable resemblance to Our Lady of Guadalupe . . . Large crowds . . . try to see the vision on the backside of highway signs. 'There appears to be a red glow around the shape.' The blotchy images . . . seem to match traditional paintings of Guadalupe, whose star spangled mantle and gown of prism colors is backlighted by a glowing outline." *Some in Washington Find Direction in Visions of the Virgin, The Santa Fe New Mexican.*

7.

Genesis 2, 3

8.

Exodus 2:1-7, *The Pentateuch and Haftorahs*, Edited by Dr. J. H. Hertz, C.H., *The Soncino Press* (5325-1975).

Moses: Prophet, Prince or Phony? Arnold Jacob Wolf, *Hadassah Magazine.*

9.

"The poets who sing of life without remembering its agony/Are fools or liars." *Hungerfield*, Robinson Jeffers

10.

"In our DNA is a history of genetic heritage which includes not only our human ancestors but also our chimpanzee ancestors, our fish ancestors, and our protozoan ancestors, going all the way to LUCA (an acronym for "last universal common ancestor") — a thermophilic bacterium that lived some four billion years ago, whose DNA all living things share . . . " *The Tree of Me*, John Seabrook, *The New Yorker.*

11.

"A 20-year old Santa Fe woman apparently took her life early on Valentine's Day by walking onto Interstate 25 near St. Francis Drive, where she was hit by at least two cars." *Woman Killed by Walking on I-25*, Santa Fe New Mexican.

12.

"The Sea of Faith was once, too, at the full, and round earth's shore lay like the folds of a bright girdle furled. But now I only hear its melancholy, long, withdrawing roar, retreating to the breath of the night-wind down the vast edges drear and naked shingles of the world . . . " *Dover Beach*, Matthew Arnold.

"And God blessed them, saying: 'Be fruitful, and multiply, and fill the waters in the seas, and let the fowl multiply in the earth.'" Genesis 1:22.

"The bit of truth behind all this — one so eagerly denied — is that men are not gentle, friendly creatures wishing for love, who simply defend themselves if they are attacked, but that a powerful

measure of desire for aggression has to be reckoned as part of
their instinctual endowment . . . Civilized society is perpetually
menaced with disintegration through this primary hostility of
men towards one another . . . Hence . . . its ideal command to
love one's neighbor as oneself, which is really justified by the fact
that nothing is so completely at variance with original human
nature as this. [but] Those who love fairy-tales do not like it
when people speak of the innate tendencies of mankind towards
aggression, destruction, and, in addition, cruelty. For God has
made them in his own image . . . In view of these difficulties,
it is expedient for every man to make humble obeisance on
suitable occasions in honor of the high-minded nature of men;
it will assist him to become universally beloved and much
shall be forgiven unto him on account of it." *Civilization and Its
Discontents*, Freud

13.

Paul Revere's Ride, Henry Wadsworth Longfellow.

Doctor Faustus, Sc. 14, Christopher Marlowe.

Genesis 1, 2

The Aeneid, Book II, Virgil.

O Captain, My Captain, Walt Whitman

Genesis 11:1-9

Julius Caesar, Act IV, line 217, William Shakespeare.

14.

"Blind ash . . . " "slid in the chasm . . . " *Give Your Heart to the
Hawks*, Robinson Jeffers.

This book of poetry has been printed on acid-free paper.
The typeface is Bernard modern Standard.

▲

Printed in the United States
99839LV00004B/589-636/A

9 780865 346109

"Blind ashes . . ." *Ossian's Grave*, Robinson Jeffers.

"Old urned ashes . . ." *The Broadstone*, Robinson Jeffers.

"The peace of the dead is dearer than gold, no one can rob you . .
." *In the Hill at New Grange*, Robinson Jeffers.

"The Brain Behind the Genius," Vicky Hallet, *Secrets of Genius,
U.S. News & World Report, Special Collector's Edition.*

15.

"The world is too much with us; late and soon,
Getting and spending, we lay waste our powers;
Little we see in Nature that is ours;
We have given our heart away, a sordid boon!"
The World Is Too Much With Us, William Wordsworth.

"All the world's a stage,/ and all the men and women merely
players:/ They have their exits and their entrances,/ And one man
in his time plays many parts, His acts being seven ages." *As You
Like It*, Act II, Scene VII, Lines 139-143, William Shakespeare.

"And Jesus, walking by the sea of Galilee, saw two brethren . . .
casting a net into the sea: for they were fishers. And he saith
unto them, Follow me, and I will make you fishers of men." St.
Matthew 4:18-19

". . . and he cast the tables out of his hands, and broke them
beneath the mount."
Exodus 32:19.

16.

"The poets who sing of life without remembering its agony/Are
fools or liars." *Hungerfield*, Robinson Jeffers.